The Endurance of Hope

Art • Poems • Stories

by

Melanie Gendron

1st WORLD PUBLISHING

1st WORLD
PUBLISHING

SAN FRANCISCO ❖ FAIRFIELD ❖ DELHI

The Endurance of Hope

Copyright ©2025 by Melanie Gendron

1st World Library
PO Box 2211
Fairfield, IA 52556
www.1stworldpublishing.com

Book & Cover Design
Melanie Gendron
melaniegendron999@gmail.com

Cover and Title Page Art
Cover: *Transition*
Title Page: *The Changeling*
Melanie Gendron

Interior Art, Photos, Illustrations
Melanie Gendron

Author Photo
Author and Bianco, author's photos

First Edition

Library of Congress Cataloging-in-Publication Data

ISBN: 978-1-4218-3568-6

In Gratitude
for this Life's journey
and for all who dare to Love

Benediction

May we be on fire
with a song of Life
as a tribe in Harmony.

May we flow like water
with the rhythms of Nature,
and dance in Union.

May our hearts take flight
with unconditional Love,
expressing our Divinity.

May we honor our Earth walk,
drawn toward Compassion, Peace,
and Gratitude for Blessings.

A Walk Within

Preface

I love
how words
make music,
craft pictures.
Yet sometimes
I have to reach
for them.

I could not find
what cuts grass.
Hours later,
lawn mower
revealed with
"Ah ha, that's it!"

Thought I'd better
write my stories
before I forget them.

Note

These stories are inspired by my life,
and I use creative license
in the telling.

Contents

Preface

Benediction

Papa's Little Princess 1

Duchess and Chicky 3

Father Unknown 5

Beginning Life Mastery 101 6

Beige, the Piddling Cocker 7

Guillotine 9

5:00 AM 10

My Most Precious Pet 11

Mother – Daughter 14

Collage and Her Kittens 17

From Dolls to Dresses 19

A Taste of Bliss 23

Bird 25

Beatle Bedlington 27

Pet Dramedy 29

Sweat Lodge 31

Art Exhibit 33

A Gift of Cinnamon 34

Jai Guru Dev, Maharishi 36

A Later Dive at Point Lobos 37

Scorpion and Dolphin 38

I Wish I Had Asked Him 39

What if I Had Treated My Husbands as Pets? 40

Impossible Love 42

Wolf and Raven 44

Dancing with a Demon 47

Mother Earth 48

Christ Light 50

The Bubble 51

Minuit 53
A Requiem for Bandit 55
Healer Cat Bianco 57
Thank God 58
Dragonflies 59
Hot Date 60
Solitude 61
The Princess of Swords 63
Cello Phonics 65
The Heart of Dance 66
Number Three Tree 68
After He Died 69
Steve and Ruditu 70
Henri 72
Henri Finds a Home 73
Blessing or Gift 74
Lament of an Elder 75
Mountain on Fire 76
Stormy Holiday 81
Deep Grey Agape 82
Gaia's Tears 83
A Domestic Feline Manifesto 84
The Vast Quiet 85
What Now? 86
Ruminating with Henri 87
If Only I Could Replay that Day 88
In My Room 90
Revelation 91
Why Can't We 92
On Awakening Gratitude 93
The Endurance of Hope 94
Acknowledgements 97
About the Author 99
Publications 100

Melanie on *The Gendron Tarot* Ace of Cups

Papa's Little Princess

I was born in a home for unwed mothers. An anxiety-fed fetus, I leapt – tight contractions down a dark, wet tunnel – I burst into a scream of light. Being touched felt safe enough to forget the journey.

I retrieved my earliest memory during a counseling session where I recalled how I felt inside the womb – anxious and insecure, my unwed mother's emotions. Not knowing the father, my origin was a mystery.

One story claims that Papa drove from Beverly to Jamaica Plain upon hearing his oldest daughter had given birth to a baby girl. He burst into the unwed mothers' home bellowing, "No one adopts my first grandchild but me!"

Rita tried to nurse me for the first few weeks. She was young, and motherhood was not planned, so she moved back to Boston. Left as a baby, I believed I was the youngest child of a large family. Papa and Mama's names placed on the birth certificate made me legally theirs. They loved me, and I became their precious pet.

I was Papa's "little princess." He told stories of world travels when he was a sailor in the Navy, and then in the Merchant Marine. As he spoke, he got a look of longing for past freedom. With a brief touch of oedipus complex, I thought that when I grew up, I could be his partner and encourage him to travel.

He was a fireman, home two days a week. The rest of the time, he slept at the station. I felt like a proud princess when he arranged firetruck maneuvers in front of our house. It made me briefly popular in the neighborhood.

On his days off, he often fished to help feed the family. He trusted me to deliver fish to the cat lady up the street and bring home the money.

Pleasing Papa made me happy; besides, he might take me out for ice cream.

Mama knew everything even though she was illiterate. She had to leave school in the third grade to work at a mill and help her impoverished family. Her Blackfoot grandmother taught her shamanic healing arts.

At six years old, I stepped on a horseshoe crab at Lynch Park beach.It cut my toe to the bone. A line of blood on the sand alerted a lifeguard I admired. She lifted me up and carried me to the beach office. My foot was wrapped and family called to bring me to the emergency room for stitches.

Instead, I was brought home where Mama bandaged my toe with a mysterious salve she concocted. A week later, I was running around due to her magic, and to this day, I am not sure which toe was cut ... no scar.

Mama called me her "little saint" when she held me in the rocking chair by the wood stove. I often kneeled with her on the kitchen floor to recite the rosary. We followed a priest on the radio, and she talked to me about her conversations with Jesus.

I loved my grandparents. For me, they were my parents. They were "spare the rod and spoil the child" old school, and "little pitchers have big ears" which meant "go away, adults only." I felt loved, my needs met, and safe.

They passed much too young: Papa when I was seven, Mama when I was ten. I grieved deeply for them and was unable to shed tears. In my teens, I visited Mama's grave, and I finally cried.

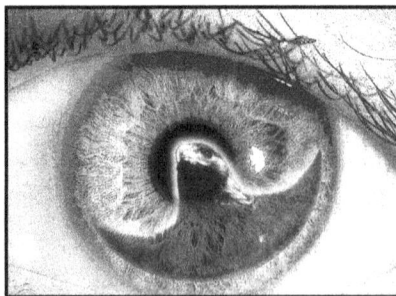

Eagle Eye

Duchess and Chicky

Sunday dinner was a family affair with fresh produce from our garden, and often, one of Papa's chickens from the coup. Mama made her irresistible delicacies on a wood stove and the smell of gourmet treats filled the house. I helped pick apples for Mama's amazing pies, and our black cocker spaniel, Duchess, entertained the family as she danced around the kitchen table. She begged for scraps, jumping on her hind legs, and her acrobatic antics evoked my laughter, sitting in a highchair.

I felt secure on Mama's lap rocking by the warm stove, snuggled into her soft breasts that fed eight babies. Duchess lay beside us, just far enough away to avoid the rocking chair, but close enough to be part of the pack.

We ran around the yard in rainstorms, and Duchess barked at the rain. She yelped when I climbed the big oak tree in our front yard. Wagging her tail, she jumped on me when I descended.

At five years old, I fit into a small cave formed by the weight of flowers curving thin branches on our forsythia bush. I had a small step stool inside where I sat in delicious solitude, with Duchess by my side. I told her my secrets while we listened to nature hum along with bees sipping the yellow nectar.

I had not begun school. It would be years before I studied philosophy, but I knew something in those moments we shared that I'd forget on occasion. I was present. Every color was bright. The sun shone through glowing petals. Each sound was distinctive, beautiful in its own way while merging in symphony.

A song of childhood vibrated my heart. Playing with my dog delighted my senses. Sometimes I picked a forsythia branch for Mama to tell her about the bees and show her how beautiful yellow is.

One day, Mama, Papa and I were sitting on the front porch stoop when our neighbor came over in tears. He had run over

Duchess. She was hiding under his car unseen. Mama who never did, wept. Even though I'd not lost a loved one before, I too cried. "Duchess is in Heaven now," meant she was no longer with me.

I asked Mama for another dog and was told no. "You're too young to care for one. Besides, I've grieved enough for pets and can't bear to lose one again."

We had chickens until Leech Street was incorporated into the town of Beverly. Not able to have a dog, I adopted one of the chicks and named her Chicky. I visited her daily on return from school. She became my confidant until the cherished chicken counselor mysteriously disappeared one afternoon.

When I asked Papa where Chicky was, he said, "On the table. Chickens are for food." The lesson was not to get too attached to animals we eat.

Horrified in that moment, I decided to become a vegetarian. Of course, that resolve did not last. Mama's cooking was irresistible.

Father Unknown

I was seven when Papa died. Photos from that time picture a sad child longing for her father. At the wake, my sister held me tight, smelling like the beer Papa drank. She kept repeating, "Now you can come live with me," as I tried to wiggle off her lap.

Confused, I asked Mama the next day why Rita said that. She answered, "Because she's your mother."

"Then, why aren't I living with her?"

Mama was brief, "Because she can't care for you."

Everything changed in that moment. My parents were my grandparents, and my sister was my mother. I had to adapt to the mystery of not knowing my actual father, but I grieved the dad who cherished his little princess, my loving Papa.

I watched him go from a handsome hero to a frail, weak old man dying in his early fifties. Then I learned that he was not my father, leaving no answer to the question, "Who is my daddy?"

My sister-mother said my father was the nephew and namesake of actor, Alfred E. Lunt, and that he died in the war. Her sister, Blanche, told me much later that Buddy Lunt had attempted to date each of the four beautiful Gendron sisters after deflowering my inebriated mother, and that she was most likely date raped.

Not knowing my patriarchal lineage, I had my DNA done to determine ethnicity. Attempting to know myself more, I searched ancestral history. I knew the matriarchal lineage – French and Native American, the Blackfoot tribe according to family. The result was: 50% European Jewish, 42% French, and 8% "other regions."

Jewish did not surprise; it elucidates my natural attraction to Kabbalah, Tarot, and mysticism. It also helps me understand a recurring teenage dream of being in a concentration camp.

Beginning Life Mastery 101

After Mama and Papa died,
I made no waves.
I feared to be a state ward
like my cousin.

I longed for family,
a reason to be alive,
things to do, people to please,
the sound of parental praise.

Aspiring perfection,
insecure, I wondered –
have I had been seeded
to the wrong planet?

When will the
Mother Ship
rescue me?

Rose Angel

Beige, the Piddling Cocker

My first day at Prince School, I sat behind a pretty girl I hoped would be a friend. She had the same "I am new" look to her. During a prescribed bathroom break, we both stood up and asked the other to partner in the lavatory line.

Deanna, "Dee," and I have been friends our whole lives since. She became the sister an only child did not have. Like her goddess counterpart, Diana, Dee has had a dog or two with her most of her life. I had a dog vicariously through her.

She cared for a younger brother while her mother worked as a club hostess. Like me, Dee had experienced childhood trauma. Her parents divorced, and she was placed for two years in an orphanage. She was now old enough to help her mom, so they had an apartment in Back Bay, Boston.

I had just moved in with my mother-sister, Rita, who worked as a waitress, sharing the restaurant profession like Dee's mother. I had left the small town of Beverly for the great city of Boston. My grandmother died, and life changed.

Making friends with Dee and her dog, Beige, helped make a difficult transition enjoyable. Her dog reminded me of my black cocker, Duchess, even though Beige was champagne colored. She was affectionate like my dog was, but she did not dance around the table like Duchess.

Dee and I played in an abandoned apartment in her building, doing improvisation, setting up altars, and playing priestess. Beige joined in wanting her belly rubbed. Laughter filled our play days. Dee eventually would become an accomplished professional actress and singer in Hollywood, graduating from Pasadena Playhouse on scholarship. But we were just having fun then, playing, and projecting futures while walking Beige.

We took ballet lessons together. We traveled on the subway, then walked to class along the Esplanade to be near the Charles River.

One day a young man gesticulated strange gestures at us, wiggling his tongue. We thought perhaps he had something wrong with him. As we crossed the overpass, he approached us saying, "Girls like what I can do for them with my tongue."

Dee was the perfect actress as she waved at a woman across the street pretending she was her mother. The man moved rapidly away. Of course, she told her mom about the incident when she got home, with her leaving ballet class as the result.

I attempted to attend class by myself but chose to quit after having my buttocks grabbed on the subway. Rita felt it to be the best decision as well, emphasizing, "Dee dances on toe shoes, and you on snowshoes." I let go the dream of becoming a prima ballerina. I was dyslexic and often went left when the class went right.

Dee moved to 306 Broadway in Cambridge, and I crossed the Harvard Bridge from Boston to Cambridge to stay overnight cuddling with Beige. We watched runners in the Boston marathon cross the finish line from a ladies lounge in the Hotel Lennox. We baked marble cakes that were as hard as marble, and we played with Beige who piddled with excitement when Dee opened her door to visitors.

Beige

Guillotine

I remember waking sweat-drenched, dreaming and fearful of the French revolution. My family had retired to our summer palace in the Alsace-Lorraine in the hope of avoiding the murderous crowd. Aristocracy was doomed in the rebellious political climate.

I descend the staircase to the vestibule and great room with my poodle by my side. Family members and staff are cowering, anxiously aware that we have been found.

The crowd is pounding on our front door. I stop mid-stair in front of our coat of arms emblazoned with three fleur-de-lis. The door bursts open, and as the mad murderers rush in, I know I am on my way to the guillotine.

One night, shaken by this recurring teenage nightmare, I told my mother about the dream. At the point where I stopped on the stair, my mother described the coat of arms on the wall beside me, and the sweeping staircase that would enhance any princess descending to the great hall.

I asked my mother how she knew what my palace looked like, and she replied, "I had the same dream, but I am with the angry crowd outside, bursting through your door."

5:00 AM

He left at 4:00 AM. At 5:00 AM, she was born – coming out of me, her body shape seen as she exited my womb. I turned to the nurse as she placed our newborn on my chest, "My husband should be here."

> Winter snow on trees,
>
> Spring's conception has been born.
>
> Baby seeks my breast.

Triptych of Sandi at Twelve

My Most Precious Pet

Pregnant in my late teens, I had a choice – have a baby or have an abortion. Bob offered to pay for the procedure, but I chose to remain pregnant, telling him, "You don't have to marry me. I want to have this baby. I can raise her on my own."

My mother disagreed. She begged him to marry me, so he proposed. I was three months pregnant when we drank alcohol to bolster our confidence and went off to the Justice of the Peace.

After the ceremony, we had a one-night honeymoon at a local motel. I was exhausted, retiring early while Bob enjoyed another woman's company in the bar. He joined me at 3:00 AM.

Bob was a gifted disciple of Don Juan, and our marriage was doomed from the beginning. I met him in art school where he was both student and model. Bob resembled Kirk Douglas, my favorite actor at the time, who played Vincent Van Gogh in *Lust for Life*. Van Gogh was my favorite artist then, so I could not keep my eyes off Bob.

One afternoon at the student hangout, we talked and he invited me to his studio apartment. Conversing and kissing for hours, I stayed the night, experiencing my first consensual lovemaking in which I felt "in love" and very present.

That morning I experienced a tingle throughout my body, exclaiming, "I will love having your baby." That statement did not go over very well, but three weeks later, having missed my period, I was pregnant. Though divorce was inevitable, I am forever grateful for the beloved daughter we made. She brought deep lessons and joy to my life.

Cassandra, nicknamed Sandi, made herself known shortly after entering my womb. Her energy was that of her namesake and Grecian prophetess. Like her, Sandi's clear vision was not always well received.

Our hearts beat together as we embarked on a deeply loving, complicated, and enlightening life share.

Very expressive, with the soul of an artist, the sharp mind of a scientist, and humor like a female Robin Williams, she made me laugh until my belly ached. I have many joyful moments remembering my most precious pet, my cherished and only child.

Looking through journals, I found a dream about her. I dreamt that Sandi and I were caught in swirling surf, going under. Like a mother whale, I pushed her to the surface. Unable to hold my breath any longer, Sandi grabbed my hand and pulled me free, able to breathe, out of water into air. The dream served as a metaphor for how we helped each other avoid drowning in waves of overwhelm.

She was diagnosed in her twenties with a rare blood condition, essential thrombocythemia, that can evolve into acute myeloid leukemia. Treatment did not work, neither chemo at Stanford, nor cannabis later at home.

How she handled her challenge was amazing – her bravery, soul growth, strength, her loving concern of others, especially me and her husband, Scott. He was her 24/7 caregiver, a most loving and attentive mate, by her side when she passed.

My heart aches knowing that I was not allowed to see her at Stanford. I was nearing the end of four and a half years of wearing an ostomy bag along with numerous intestinal operations. She had no immune system, and the bag outgassed. I could only call her daily to tell her I was praying for a miracle, and I loved her.

After the reconnection surgery was done, and the bag removed, I was finally able to visit her at home. She was on hospice. We had a few hours together, with her bald crown missing the luxurious hair she once had down to her waist. She was still beautiful, but obviously ill.

She died two days later, before I could see her in person again. I connected with her spirit while meditating, and I reacted to the morphine she took to manage extreme pain. Her husband called to tell me that she passed at 5:00 PM, but I already knew because my reaction to morphine had ceased. I had said my goodbye, wishing I could join her.

During our brief visit, I told Sandi that being her mother was a privilege. She replied, "It's been a privilege all the way around." Her statement was all-inclusive, and everyone who knew her carries a touch of her light inside.

Portrait of Sandi at Twelve

Mother – Daughter

She said she would never grow old as lovely as me.
Named after Cassandra, she was prophetic.

There were days we loved deeply
like best friends,
and times of dissention –
songs of mother and daughter.

She was fearless with the truth
as she saw it.

She confronted me with accusations
of neglect and lack of acknowledgment.
She said, "You never listen,"
then marveled at how my love for her
was unconditional.

She thought we were
soulmates through time –
mother, daughter, sister, brother.

I admit I've lived in my
head a long time –
making art, seeking spirit,
propelled by the longing
to communicate with God.

Did I really miss her need to be heard?
I did listen. I tried to understand.

Motherhood is a demanding job.
No matter how hard you juggle,
eggs will fall.

Career both supports and separates.
Loneliness is inevitable
for an only child.

Every day consumed
with meditating and creating.
I worked long hours to supply our needs.
Did I sometimes fail her need?

I miss her calling me out.
She remains a beautiful young woman
forever now –
never to grow old
like her loving mother.

Cassandra as The Queen of Heaven

Portrait of Collage

Collage and Her Kittens

My three-year-old daughter and I lived in a small Cambridge walk-up, second floor. Coming home with groceries and a toddler, I did not notice the calico kitten who followed us up the stairs until I turned to close the door.

I left it open to offer the alley cat a home. Obviously intelligent, she came inside. I named her Collage to celebrate the beautiful blend of her three colors – yellow, rust, and black.

We lived in that apartment for a couple of years, and Collage raised two litters of kittens under my bed. The second litter had a grey kitten that Sandi insisted was hers. She picked him up in her chubby, little hands and dropped him.

I tried to explain why I was burying her kitty. "Grey Kitty died and went to cat heaven, and he is all right." None of that meant anything. She was only three, and mad at me for taking her cat away.

Collage took it all in stride, giving extra attention to her remaining brood. The four kittens – black Midnight, orange Sunny, calico Patches, and tabby Tiger – grew into vary adoptable felines. Her first brood found homes quickly.

Allergy testing revealed a sensitivity to cats. Even though Collage had borne two litters, I decided she needed a new home.

I was working as head fashion designer for The Hammond Kroll Design Workshop in Cambridge, Massachusetts, spending summers creating fashions and producing shows on Martha's Vineyard. I relied on husband Bob to give Collage to friends who loved her, and find homes for the kittens. Instead, he took the cats to the SPCA. Collage may have been euthanized. Disappointment with Bob grew with yet another uncaring act.

I prayed for the cat and her kittens, and pictured them in loving homes with appreciative people who cared enough to adopt a rescue. It helped assuage the guilt of having to let them go.

Portrait of Cassandra as Sun Goddess

From Dolls to Dresses

I

While visiting with my cousin, Jeanie, in Salem, she asked her daughter to bring out the Barbie collection. I had designed and hand-sewn elaborate costumes for her mother's dolls when I was a teenager, with each stitch equal in size.

One by one, seven Barbies in Melanie designs paraded down the table runway:

    French Renaissance Barbie in her ruffled beige gown
        with hot pink roses,
    Oriental Barbie in a shimmering silver kimono adorned
        with purple irises,
    Country Barbie wearing a long, red plaid skirt and
        fringed leather jacket,
    Hippie Barbie in a flowing, multi-colored maxi-dress
        with flowers in her hair,
    Princess Barbie in a bright pink ensemble edged in gold
        with sequins,
    Bewitched Barbie in a sensual, black satin gown and
        star-studded witch hat, and
    Bride Barbie in a classic white tulle gown, long lace train,
        crystal tiara and sparkling veil.

II

I lived around the corner from the Hammond Kroll Design Workshop in Cambridge. There were piles of discounted fabrics from which I made clothes for my daughter and me. Skill improved, and my mother asked to make a dress for a friend to wear to her daughter's wedding.

Laurie was plump, and the Kelly-green, full-skirted dress with matching sleeve-length cape she insisted upon made her look fat. I refunded her money. It was a valuable, as well as expensive, lesson – to trust my instincts as designer and steer clients away from anything that does not enhance them.

III

Sixty-nine-year-old Hammond had been a furniture designer along with Eames. Kroll furniture was displayed at the Guggenheim Museum. He became a mentor, displaying fashions I made to sell in the workshop's store. Though I was self-taught, he offered me the job of head designer.

We drove to New York in Hammond's Austin-Healey convertible to find fabrics even in winter. I put on fashion shows for the workshop in Boston and New York, with designs appearing in *Women's Wear Daily*. Two summers were spent on Martha's Vineyard producing shows at the Edgartown Inn where the Kennedys congregated.

The last runway show for the workshop was a benefit for WGBH-TV. I designed twelve ensembles based on the Horoscope. My actress friend, Dee, read the poetic Zodiacal fashion descriptions, and the band played music titled Tapestry to honor the show's title of the same name.

IV

After the workshop, I was on my own designing for individual clients. One of them, Beth, was gaining her PhD in business at Harvard. Impressed with my talent and aware of my circumstance, she asked her Dow Chemical CEO father for funds to run a fashion business promoting my designs.

Melanie Designs accomplishments included: a popular Zodiac line to east coast boutiques and the Bahamas, a line in Finnish fabrics for the Apogee Boutique on Newbury Street in Boston, and fashions for a black models' runway at the Boston's Prudential Center in support of the NAACP. My designs for Tenneco Advanced Materials were featured at New York Fashion Week with various fashion designers, including Bill Blass.

V

I moved on to painting and print making while retaining interest in fashion. Costumed segments were created by invitation for two wearable art exhibits at the Art Museum of Santa Cruz County. The first celebrated Byzantine art with a triptych of arches having stained glass windows. They were large enough to house the three models who paraded single file down the aisle onto the stage, each to her own arch. The second celebrated my Blackfoot ancestry with models in fashions inspired by Native American culture, dancing to flute and drum.

VI

Hammond Kroll said I would look back on my fashion years with great fondness. He was right. I savor the memories while making new ones. Always – making new ones.

Angel Bride

M and TM

A Taste of Bliss

While working for the Hammond Kroll Design Workshop, and during running Melanie Designs, I was spiritually seeking. Hatha Yoga became a daily practice. Kirpal Singh was my Yoga teacher's guru. The gallery owner, whose shows I hung, also followed him. Plans were made for my initiation. Unfortunately, Kirpal Singh passed away before that could happen.

I decided to meditate with "Om" as my mantra. That proved too powerful when I found myself in an ethereal tunnel, hearing angels sing. Approaching the light ahead, I held back, afraid to die.

I desired a teacher who could guide meditation safely. I did Tratak, candle gazing, with Dale who had meditated for a year on the edge of a volcano on Hawaii. His energy was palpable, and I had visions of his many lives, tracing him back to a battle on the fields of Sparta. I smelled spilled blood and ended the session.

Dale said I was a natural intuitive and offered to introduce me to his coven leader, a woman who had some fame as a Boston psychic. My inner voice cautioned that my ego could grow too large in his group. I wanted someone like Kirpal Singh.

One of the artists from the Museum School, Ken, told me about Maharishi Mahesh Yogi. He and a group of artists were going to study with Maharishi in the Himalayas. I felt a longing I knew could not be fulfilled yet. I lacked the money, and Sandi's needs came first, no matter what.

Ken said that I could receive a mantra and training in Transcendental Meditation in Cambridge as he was hosting Jerry Jarvis, Maharishi's United States ambassador. Offered student rates, I signed up and encouraged Bob to learn T.M. also.

My moment arrived, and I was ushered into a quiet room with a puja altar set up. I had prepared as I was told, avoiding any drugs or alcohol for weeks.

Jerry Jarvis officiated. The smell of incense and a depth of silence filled the room. He whispered my mantra, had me repeat it back to him, then said it was private, not to be vocalized, heard only internally.

I was left to meditate, following his instructions. I quickly experienced an absence of thought and a wondrous sense of well-being. I knew this was what I wanted, what my daily spiritual practice was missing, what nuns had not been able to give.

Maharishi came to Cambridge for a lecture two weeks later. I sat in the front row of the auditorium, right where I could easily see the guru. He entered the stage, sat in lotus, and began talking.

I transcended, and when I became aware of the room, everyone including Maharishi was gone. Maharishi's aura was powerful, and I had blissed out. I've meditated every day since.

The Mocking Bird

Bird

The young bird flapped his wings trying to fly. He fell from the tree in a parking lot where his parents built their nest. The hard cement hurt his claws as he hopped and cheeped in fear. The nest was an impossible flight, and he had seen strange creatures get inside metal boxes from his perch high in his home tree.

I saw him on the way to my car. I took plates painted with images of basil, rosemary and thyme out of their box to make a temporary cage. Later, I placed him in a plush birdcage, covered with a blanket at night, safe in a new home.

I thought he was a sparrow, and for a couple of days, I brought him seeds that he could not eat. He didn't know how to tell me what he needed. I consulted an ornithologist to identify him. He was a fledgling mockingbird who could mimic every bird song. He required a diet of ground beef, calcium from eggshells, and meal worms. I fed him every two hours, to his loud calls while he shook his wings. He taught me how to respond to him in his language, singing a high-pitched *chick, chick, chick.* I named him Bird.

His personality captivated everyone in the family – me, his surrogate mother, my husband, Dick, and daughter, Sandi. As he grew, we encouraged him to fly throughout the house so he could learn to catch insects. One day, he thought the glint in my eye was a bug. I wore a patch for a few days after, looking like a pirate. Dive bombing the dog was his favorite pastime, though Beatle did not like the game, running for cover.

Bird liked to fly from shoulder to shoulder singing a variety of sounds. His songs increased as he listened to other birds in the backyard feeding station. A mocker settled in the coffee tree outside, and Bird spent long teenage moments singing to her. I knew that as much as I loved him, he was a protected species that needed to return to the wild. However, I wanted to keep him as long as possible. Certain rooms with doors to the outside were off-limits.

One day, Sandi's friend came to the unblocked kitchen door, and Bird flew out. It was time, but I grieved, calling to him with *chick, chick, chick*. He settled on the right side of the house through the winter, opposite the mocker in the coffee tree. Both thrived with suet and food at the backyard station. They shared their songs, and the clamor of many birds kept them company.

In the spring, Bird and the mocker he longed for mated. They raised six healthy chicks, nesting in the coffee tree. I watched them become fledglings, flapping their wings to leave the parents who remained together for life. Bird taught me a much-needed lesson – to be authentic and strive for a life desired. He filled my heart with joy singing, *chick, chick, chick*.

Bird was my favorite avian rescue. He became a symbol for freedom of self-expression and honoring one's true nature. Not too long after Bird flew out to his life purpose, Dick and I divorced.

Years later, I was visiting a possible mate in Chapel Hill, North Carolina. As we walked to his car, I noticed a mocker on a branch above us. I called to the bird with *chick, chick, chick*, and he flew down to a fence just inches from me and sang his symphony. My friend observed in his southern drawl, "My, my, you can charm a bird right out of its tree!"

I thanked Bird for teaching me his song.

Beatle

Beatle Bedlington

My daughter was an only child as I had been, and like me, she learned to entertain herself. I always wanted a dog, and figured Sandi could benefit from playing with a pet. Researching dogs that were hypoallergenic, I saw a Bedlington terrier and fell for the breed. I found a reputable breeder in a nearby town and arranged a visit. Dick drove Sandi and me to consider a new family member.

The liver-colored female I coveted was destined to be a show dog and not for sale. The two available puppies were male. The pup named Ziggy chose us. Dick paid $360.00, a steep price at the time, but I felt the adorable zig-zag puppy was worth it.

On the way home, I asked Sandi to pick a name for her puppy. She was quiet, so Dick and I suggested names – Duke, Fido, Scout, or maybe keep Ziggy? Then I said, "Beatle – you love the Beatles, Sandi, how about Beatle?" The name stuck. Dick and I were quite happy with our choice. We thought we had pleased Sandi who remained very quiet the whole ride home. Years later she confided that she hated the name and disliked the dog.

Beatle needed to be trained and housebroken, requiring the involvement a puppy demands. He came down with distemper. When I told the breeder, she said she would give us another pup if Beatle died. I spent a week following the veterinarian's instructions, pushing huge pills down the puppy's gullet. He needed almost all my attention, and Sandi resented her new sibling.

He became my dog, and of course, I loved him. He was neutered, but still humped. Sandi became a favorite for him to tackle which made him even less appealing to her.

Beatle perceived Sandi as a playmate. On her return home from school, he jumped on her and pulled her to the floor. He wanted to play after spending a morning running wild through the woods, and he had learned her return time. Sometimes Sandi would play, sometimes be annoyed, calling him gross.

I had a different outcome in mind than what happened. Like many parents, I projected my unfulfilled childhood desires onto my child, wanting to make her life better than mine had been.

Beatle missed Rose Valley where he had been able to run through the woods. Our new house was across from a county building, and we had to obey leash laws. Dick made our dog a run across the yard. Beatle barked as he ran which the neighborhood did not appreciate. I suspect the bird feeding station I kept in winter was too loud also.

Beatle developed tumors that required surgery, then grew back to become inoperable as they encompassed his lungs. He came to me for petting, and hung by my side. One night, I noticed how my energy flowed into him, possibly extending his life. His breathing was shallow, and I knew I should let him go with gratitude, "Sweet boy, thank you for the years we've shared. If you need to go, I am ready." He died at nine-years-old that night. He was buried in the back yard, and we all felt very close at the burial – even Sandi cried.

I was more complete with a dog in the family – and gerbils, mice, birds. Caring for creatures grows compassion.

Sandi rescued many cats in her adult years. I believe she learned her lesson well, even though we named the dog Beatle.

Mousekin

Pet Dramedy

Sandi named her beloved mouse Mousekin. She took the mouse everywhere. Hiding under her long hair, it sat on her shoulder. I noticed Mousekin while shopping for groceries and told Sandi to leave her at home. She could jump off the shoulder and cause havoc in a store. Yet on another shopping day, Mousekin peaked out again. Sandi had ignored my request. A shopper saw the white vermin and squealed. Sandi, Mousekin, and I were promptly escorted from the store.

We added a hamster Sandi named Hamfa to our menagerie. He tended to bite, and she lost interest. Hamfa eventually escaped his cage and wandered wild throughout the house, hiding in ducts. He killed Mousekin to get at her food. We buried the cherished mouse, then placed a "Have a Heart" cage to catch Hamfa. I took the hamster to the commuter train station at the end of our street and released the murderous creature to the wild. For all I know, he mated with some related vermin and bore a whole new species.

Gifted with two gerbils at six years old, Sandi kept them in her room, promising to keep the cage clean. She did a good job with an occasional assist. One of the gerbils was pregnant, though we had been told they were both male. Having a cage-load of gerbils was drama enough until my daughter swung the male in a circle over her head while dancing. His tail came off in her hand as he flew across the room. We found him, then procured the gerbils a new home.

Ratquela Welchade, the sixth-grade rat mascot, spent the summer months with us. She was a marvelous rat, extremely affectionate, having been cuddled by many classmates.

We had a parakeet named Budgie who died when my husband's Australian colleague visited. Standing over the cage,

Brian asked the bird, "How are you doing, mate?" And Budgie, perhaps homesick, keeled over and died.

I kept a bird feeding station year-round, becoming known as the bird lady. You could hear the birds a couple of streets away. During spring mating season, neighborhood children brought wounded chicks to me for healing care. Some made it, some did not. A robin was recovering well, so Sandi named him Robby. A few days later, he passed away, reminding us of Collage's grey kitten that toddler Sandi accidentally dropped. Sandi was old enough now to understand the passage of something loved.

I observed my girl one sunny morning sitting in the coffee tree outside the kitchen door. A family of finches were enjoying the seed we provided. Sandi was quiet, very Zen. She put her hand forward with seed in it, and birds came to her as if she were Saint Francis. They alighted on her fingers and fed. I watched in awe with appreciation for a daughter who projected such peace. I felt reassured she would handle life's dramas with grace, especially those involving animals.

Brigitte

Sweat Lodge

I showered and entered the sweat lodge where drums swirled oppressive heat into my lungs. I lay on the floor for cooler air, and settled into the repetitive beat, ready to attract some animal allies.

I entered a tunnel – circular, ridged, yet fluidly smooth. I moved effortlessly, twisting through the earth. An otter appeared, and presented himself in various postures. Coy, he did not answer when I asked if he would return with me.

Then, a red fox eagerly upstaged Otter, whirling us around, hand in paw, while Otter banged a drum against his belly. Fox agreed to return, but Otter enjoyed his tease until he said we could hold hands for the trip back.

I was told to dance with each animal on return. Recognition secured their help. The drums played a fast roll; and circling, we traveled back rapidly through the tunnel.

Agatha, Gail and I enjoyed cooler air in the shower room as candlelight flickered, and music inspired a dance. I fluffed a fox tail to become four-legged. Reflections flickered on the wall.

Gail, whose totem is Fox, expressed her recognition.

I ran outside to the pool. My inner otter dove in fast from the deep side into perfectly tepid, silky water. I could barely contain myself rolling around, playing with a ball that floated on the surface. Women nearby laughed.

Agatha dove in, and said, "You're an otter!"

Only an Egg, America

Art Exhibit

Standing before my artwork in a group exhibit, a woman asked what I thought of the painting. "Only an Egg, America" was generously littered with eagle bones, a human baby skeleton, and the hint of democracy's death. I shrugged a "not sure" to get her honest opinion. She felt free to express, saying, "I think this artist is mentally disturbed," to which I replied, "I agree."

It reminded me of a contest in Junior High where art was chosen for an exchange program with Russia. I was proud of my painting, "Gnarled Hand with Rose and Bloody Knife," an Edgar Allen Poe inspired watercolor.

Called into the principal's office, I expected to receive the prize. Instead, I was questioned by the school psychologist and sent home with a letter for my mother.

> I am not averse to your critique of my art,
> but judge aversely your averse delivery.

The sky might not be blue.

The Critic

A Gift of Cinnamon

Once I met his seven-year-old son, I was in love. Donny had a shock of curly blond hair, a disarming smile, and a very bright mind. He lived with Don's ex-wife in Texas, spending part of his summer and holidays with his dad in California.

One day driving around Santa Cruz, Donny said he would like me to marry his dad. Don agreed, but I had reservations when told he left his first wife while pregnant with their fourth child. Uncertain about us, I broke up with him.

He gave me a cockatiel as a parting gift. I thanked him, but did not see how I could care for a bird, so he kept him. After briefly dating others, my heart ached for Don. He was a friend with whom I could talk, and my emotions were running wild. Not sure how he felt, I chanced driving to his house and waited on his doorstep until he returned home.

We reconnected – Don, the cockatiel named Cinnamon, and me. Don and I spent a few days making love in Saratoga, and my heart felt happy. Raised Catholic, we married in the Holy Cross Chapel on December twenty-first. Many of our friends from the meditation center attended. Cinnamon stayed at our new home in Santa Cruz ready to call me mama.

Transcendental Meditation played a major part in choosing each other. Shortly after we married, Maharishi called for as many sidhas as possible to join him at a month-long course in Fairfield, Iowa at Maharishi International University (MIU). Our friend David could not go because of work demands. He offered my attending in his place. I was on my way to Fairfield to be with Maharishi in winter, rather than honeymoon.

It was one of the most intensive months of my life. I housed with some students who remained lifelong friends after the course, among them talented poet and author, Diane Frank. She helped a very emotional newlywed, often crying, wishing I were home playing with Cinnamon.

The winter weather was difficult, and many of us caught a cold. Don and I talked daily as he was setting up a seminar business teaching learning techniques to students and teachers. I feared losing myself as an artist in service to his five-year plan to make our first million.

I took seriously my previous husband's comment that my art would never earn much money, and launched into co-creating Powerlearning Systems with my new husband upon returning home. The earlier marriage had affected the new one with an emotional resolve. This time I would prove my worth and be an artist also. The only caged bird in the house would be Cinnamon.

We did our T.M. Program together at the meditation center, and I belonged to a women's support group that met semimonthly. My life had routine and felt stable. Cinnamon became our bird, though he got most excited around me and my daughter, Sandi. He would enjoy standing on our hands, moving his wings as if to fly, extending them out straight in orgasmic beauty.

Growing our business took time and many hours apart with Don teaching seminars in colleges across California. Cinnamon was my bird confidant like my chicken, Chicky, had been in childhood. I confided that I was lonely, finding the artists I met in San Francisco attractive.

When we separated, the cockatiel who enjoyed sitting on our shoulders remained with Don. I saw my cinnamon-cheeked bird five days a week at work for a year after the divorce. I received an hourly pay from the seminar business to help me start over.

After I moved out, Cinnamon flew away when Don forgot he was on his shoulder and walked out on the deck. Don grieved the loss of me and his beloved bird and placed an ad in the local paper for Cinnamon. He got a call after a few days from a woman in Capitola, miles from his west side Santa Cruz home.

Cinnamon had alighted on the woman's shoulder and was very amenable when she caged him. I wondered if he flew away to find me because he missed his mama as much as I missed him.

Jai Guru Dev Maharishi

Joined –
Absolute
Infinity.

Grace emanates from
Universal consciousness –
Realigning, redefining,
Unifying all parts.

Defined, I Am
Eternally deep,
Verified, validated.

Magnified gratitude
Arises from the
Happiness of
Absolute
Reality
Inherent in the
Silence that is
Home for the
Infinite Self.

A Later Dive at Point Lobos . . .

We rode out to sea with pristine air licking the glass surface, and he was there resting in the kelp. My delight sang out, *Dear Otter, I am so happy to see you!*

He looked into my eyes and clapped his hands as he broke loose from the kelp. He rolled in the water, joy apparent. I remembered the outrageous aliveness that my swimming like an otter invoked.

Our first dive was in Bluefish Cove at ninety feet. With ears slow to acclimate, I did a gradual descent. The fluorescent rainbowed bubbles enthralled as they rose toward the surface.

Glancing upward, I saw kelp silhouetted against brilliant light streaming down like God sending illumination to a waiting Earth.

Later, I danced clever Fox and playful Otter to chants, flute and drum; and the depth of their gifts revealed. They helped channel healing purification so joy could become a palpable reality.

After many hours of aloneness, loneliness dissolved, for we were silent together –

And empowered.

Otters

Scorpion and Dolphin

We had Jyotish astrology readings with Muktananda's advisor. I asked if our marriage would endure lifelong. Chakrapani said, "Only if you make it through the next two months." Wolf showed up, and Don told me the seer warned him in a private session that if I left Don, I would have years of suffering.

In marriage counseling sessions, I was warned again to not leave my marriage. Don was advised to refrain from making me wrong, and work compassionately on our relationship.

He planned a holiday trip to Florida in the hope of saving our marriage. Entering our cabin, we were proceeded by a large scorpion which made me squeamish. It felt like a bad omen.

The trip was wonderful – especially swimming with dolphins at the Dolphin Research Center. We were told dolphins come to people who are natural in the water, who have dolphin energy.

A male dolphin took a liking to me, and I thought, *Please don't take me below the surface. I did not take a Sudafed to manage water pressure.* He offered his dorsal fin which I grabbed, and we swam around the pool surface. I was convinced he sensed my need to remain above water. Other dolphins swam around me, occasionally rubbing against my body.

There were several of us in the pool, and I was asked eventually to go to the side of the pool as dolphins were congregating around me, and other people wanted to experience swimming with them.

Don and I dove in golden waters, boated in the Everglades, and enjoyed a great vacation. Unfortunately, when we kissed, I could not get thoughts of Wolf out of my mind. On returning home, I fell into a depression, figuring that I would have to wait another year for the intimacy we shared on our holiday.

I Wish I Had Asked Him

I wish I had asked him what he meant. We were enjoying our long-postponed Hawaiin honeymoon. We started on Kawai – peaceful, beauty everywhere. We made intimate love, and I was happier than I thought anyone should be.

We hiked, snorkeled, and scuba dived. I figured someday we might settle on Hawaii, and I would paint pictures of the Pacific Ocean reefs and the seductive island beauty that inspired my heart.

On our last day, I asked him if he loved me more after sharing such a wonderful honeymoon. He answered, "I never had that infatuation for you that most people think of as being in love." Hearing this, I got chills down my spine and could not respond.

I wondered why he had married me.

Years later, after divorce, I finally asked him about his reply. He said that his love was mature love. That was what he meant by his comment. I wished I had asked him what he meant at the time.

It might have made a difference.

The Kiss

What if I Had Treated My Husbands as Pets?

The wonderful thing about pets is most are trainable. Men – not so much. Each husband attracted me to the point of falling in love, yet each had a tragic flaw.

Bob asked me not to use his last name when he offered marriage to legitimize our child. We met when I was Patricia, nickname Pat. I discovered that Melanie was my first name, not middle, when I needed my birth certificate to marry.

Bob was an attentive lover that any of the women who experienced his talent could verify. He was a Leo who enjoyed all the females in the pride. I can accept promiscuity in a pet. Collage brought various alley cats home during heat. Yet I found it unacceptable in a husband.

Dick was a brilliant scientist who wanted to be like Star Trek's Spock. Emotions were questionable and uncomfortable. He felt like cool water after being burned in a Leo's fire. We were great roommates, but emotional connection was minimal. I loved listening to him, drawn to his intellect and clean ethics. He asked me how I could put so much time into my art as it made little money. I realized he did not understand my passion. Not sharing intimate feelings was fine for me with pets, but not with my husband.

Don was a physicist and professor. We both meditated, married in the Catholic Church, and believed we would last. Building the Powerlearning Systems seminar business kept us apart, with Don traveling most weekends after working at the college all week. Lacking attention to our time together, we grew apart. I've wondered if adding a dog or cat to our family would have assuaged my loneliness.

I married in love with each man, intending to spend our lives together – either by choice or because of pregnancy. What was has past, and now is happening. I suspect that even if I had treated husbands like pets, we still would have done what we did.

In Memory of Patricia

Impossible Love

I

The distance between two is forever . . .
He, sky – She, earth
Mars craving Venus,
perfect mirrors.

Romance has conditions.
When met, lovers merge
defining their gift a blessing,
a Heavenly moment,

impossible to last
when fear's grasp
exceeds the reach
of love's connection.

II

I never stopped
loving him . . .
or the ghost of
my perception of him.

His children resented
his control.
I too – when my time came
to grow up.

I had discourse with the ghost
for lifetimes . . .
after our divorce,
through each relationship.

My heart ached
for failing the King,
or so I dreamed for too long.
It takes two to disentangle.

III

What about deciding to dance again,
merge worlds, re-create and love again?
Possible? Impossible?
You choose.

Indra's Infinite Creation

Wolf and Raven

When I first met Wolf, he wore green like the redwoods in a rainy season. His smell was honey musk, and I was taken with the depth of his eyes. He spoke in a deep baritone that stirred feelings I knew I should resist.

My daughter and her boyfriend talked with Wolf at a street fair and were impressed. He knew my name when Sandi mentioned her artist mother, saying he was aware of my work and wanted to represent me. That led to our initial meeting with Sandi and Jeff by my side.

Wolf offered a gift of Ambar, a perfume he imported from India to sell in boutiques across the country. He said it was meant for a pretty woman. I expected him to give it to my lovely daughter, but Wolf put the resin perfume on my hand, not Sandi's. I doubted that this tall, dark man who was obviously wooing me should represent my art.

Wolf spontaneously created poetry extoling my goddess virtues, and I was mesmerized. His voice was exceptionally charismatic, lulling my mind to believe whatever he said. He convinced me to make him my agent with the promise of distributing art and initiating commissions. Had I known what I was to experience, I would have run – but then, the temptation was impossible to resist.

The next week, Sandi and Jeff surprised me with a visit from Wolf while my husband was away on business. We all sat in the living room discussing a variety of subjects, as well as art. Wolf asked me if we could discuss something in private. I suggested we go out on the deck.

When I closed the door, he took me in his arms and kissed me. He said he had to do that as he was thinking about me all day every day since we met. Shaken, I insisted we rejoin my daughter and Jeff.

Subsequent business meetings occurred with kissing as part of our exchange. I rationalized that it was innocent enough, but guilt is hard to deny. I told Wolf we had to refrain from sensual play and be professional. That seemed reasonable until he cried, "I feel destined to never be with my soulmate," while holding me in a very close, emotional hug.

It was inevitable. I left my husband who said he feared Wolf was dangerous and that I would most likely suffer. I replied to his concern prophetically with, "I have to have this experience, even if it means going to Hell."

My raven self had resonated with Wolf's inner totem, and my life changed. Like Siddhartha, I was drawn into nights of ecstatic bliss with my Tantric master, dancing in unison.

Days were a daze of work traveling the west coast from Las Vegas to Portland selling art and products to galleries and boutiques.

We exhibited visionary surrealist art at expos and curated art exhibits at the Santa Cruz Art League – "Art of the Dreamtime" and "Blessingway."

The Blessingway news release was a testament to the spiritual calling that brought Wolf and me together, as well as the physical chemistry. It read:

"In all ancient cultures, there are ceremonies honoring new birth, rebirth, and passing from one world to the next. The names may differ from country to country, tribe to tribe, or with different dogmas and beliefs, yet the concept of celebration, release and transformation remains the same. We are rebirthing each day in our private lives as well as on a global perspective, and we are recreating our reality as we choose it.

"This show is in dedication to the beauty both around us and within us, and to honor life in all its forms, including the transformation called death. May we all find ways to recreate our world in the forms necessary to sustain and nourish ourselves, our Mother Planet, and all children of this Earth."

Wolf's personality changed from a lover at night to a character I called Black Bart during the day. He bullied and threatened to maintain control. Black Bart resembled Johnny Cash in his all-black attire, boots, cowboy hat, and Folsom Prison sneer.

We separated after an abusive relationship and failed business left me in emotional and financial debt. I wished Wolf well when we parted. He thanked me for my well wishes, but requested that he be left alone. There was too much failure between us.

"When I first saw you, I could not stop thinking about you, so I decided to pursue the attraction if you were open to the idea. Apparently, you were. Your loneliness was a shroud. You left a comfortable life with a husband who could provide for you for a younger man – an alternative dreamer, a champion of artists, a poet with little financial means. I warned you not to leave your marriage to be with me."

I agreed that our passion proved volatile, and like him, hoped for a more serene existence. He told me that when I frightened him, he was not accountable for his actions. He added, "It takes two to perpetuate a psychology of violence. I choose not to have you in my life. However, I wish you well, not ill, and have hopes for your growth, for your coming to open and honest terms with your shadow."

I remember the day we hiked at Pfeiffer State Park in Big Sur when Wolf led me off the path. Behind a group of trees, on the edge of a cliff overlooking the ocean, we made passionate love.

A mixture of excitement and fear defined our relationship. I had to leave because the fear became more than the excitement of being together.

I certainly learned a lot about my shadow being with Wolf. For that at least, I am grateful.

Dancing with a Demon

He was frightfully handsome,
a charismatic magnet
smart women would avoid.

He fathomed dark
secrets before I did,
found them in my attic,
stroked them alive.

Down tunnels of
forgetfulness,
lost in sensual oblivion,
my regret longed for
the life I knew before
a wolf bayed at my door.

Later, I faced the dark moon,
befriended my mirror,
and danced . . .

Memories recalled
how it felt before his agitation
sent every cell screaming,
when order prevailed.

In Pandora's box, only hope
remained after years of confusion,
layers of missions and remissions,
and belief in a calling –

so I danced.

Mother Earth

I needed to expand income and be more self-reliant. I learned a lot at the Powerlearning seminars assisting Don, who held a PhD in education. I also served at two of Lynn V. Andrew's week-long workshops in Yucca Valley, one for making shields, another for drums. Being an invited vendor and teacher boosted my self-esteem and consciousness.

I competed for a teaching position with SPECTRA, a program run by the Cultural Council of Santa Cruz County. Inspired by Lynn, I wrote a lesson plan for teaching Native American crafts to elementary students and was hired to do my program.

At Lynn's second Yucca Valley workshop, I painted participants' drums, being paid for my service. We suffered 115° heat, and the vendor hall had fans, but no air conditioning. There were few customers.

One of the vendors did massage and offered a session in exchange for one of my prints. I lay on his table and settled into the experience. I had a vision. I saw a sea of glass, and on it, ahead of me, a Being of brilliant light sat on a shining throne. "We have much to give; you just have to get out of the way."

This vision was transformative. I felt unconditional divine love and knew I could not continue despising myself for adultery, or poor choices. I had to forgive me. I was in awe throughout the vision, so did not think to ask how to get out of my own way. However, my heart knew that would reveal in time.

My first SPECTRA assignment was at Live Oak Elementary School. I dressed in the Mother Earth dress a Blackfoot designer made, a gift from Wolf. I took students out to the sunny school yard to have a Medicine Way four directions ceremony as a prelude to creating their shields incorporating fire, water, earth, and air. My students loved the fun and were inspired to create.

A Seventh Day Adventist mother witnessed my ceremony. She thought I was teaching a pagan religion to the kids. My class went up before the school board, and I was thrilled that the Cultural Council backed me. They asked if I was teaching a religion and I answered that it was play-acting to make our expressive time together kinesthetic fun. I agreed to be more academic, but I still enjoyed lecturing in the Mother Earth dress.

I taught in the SPECTRA program for a few years, at several elementary and middle schools, gathering donated materials from Saltz Tannery and utilizing pizza circles for the shields. I also taught in private schools and served as art teacher for grades kindergarten to sixth grade at Santa Cruz Montessori.

After teaching all the grades at Live Oak, I hung a shield exhibit in the large recreation room. At another school, we painted a mural in the library. I loved teaching, and figure I probably taught a few thousand children over the years, often coming down with bronchial infections in winter from exposure to runny noses.

It was worth the sacrifice.

Shield

Christ Light

It was so hot you could fry an egg on pavement.
The heat lay oppressive on my lungs.
Between wake and sleep, I envisioned eyes
of pure love and felt total acceptance.

I was suddenly home, no doubt, no fear,
inspired by Guides to guidance . . .

We have so much to give you;
you just have to get out of the way.

Bright pictures of Christ and Light pouring
forth through clouds, the hands of God . . .

Shine brighter the more you give,
and receive without attachment.
Give all concern to Me that I may reside
in grace within a willing heart.
Should you forget that we are one being, I will
wait silent for you to hear our refrain again.

No matter the challenge, I do listen
sooner or later . . . and I come Home.

The Bubble

She had no immune system and lived in a bubble.
She requested a print of my painting,
Butterfly Woman.

She said,

This image
opens up my universe
and helps me be free,
like a butterfly.

Butterfly Woman

Portrait of Minuit

Minuit

When I was three years old, my person moved to the city. I was left at Harbin Hot Springs to become prey in the woods. My neck tore when I struggled to break free from the bobcat that caught me.

I returned to the room where I once lived. There on the bed, a woman was meditating. I jumped up and settled on her lap. I felt safe when she stroked me. I made sure to stay by the room all week to be on her lap at meditation time. I knew she could be my new person.

The day she told her partner she decided to help me, I was grateful. I was feeling weak physically from the neck injury, and emotionally from being abandoned by my first person.

The lady called me by my old name, Rhianna, but I did not want that name anymore, so I did not respond. She suggested "Midnight," and I ignored her. Then she said, "How do you like 'Minuit'? That's French for Midnight, a good name for a black cat." I loved it, so I rubbed against her leg and purred. She named me – it was a sure sign that I had a new home. A visit to a veterinarian helped heal the tear on my neck.

My new person decided to keep me even though she had an allergy to cat dander. She overcame the allergy saying, "You're Mommy's sweet girl, and I will take good care of you."

Mommy and I enjoyed seventeen years together with lots of shared experiences. I was free to roam the outdoors, happy to be home at meditation time.

I had to adjust to many new places. One year after Mommy and her partner separated, I stayed with her ex-partner who had a loud voice when he was angry. I ran to the closet often to rest in my favorite hiding place.

One day I got to live full time with Mommy again. She was attending school, working, and able to rent a room for us. We moved to the Santa Cruz mountains after a couple of years, where we lived near a huge forest of redwood trees.

I never forgot being attacked in the woods. I learned to be cautious, finding special places to hide and listen to birds I might catch. I avoided dogs and most cats, and watched out for predators.

I lived out the rest of my life in the mountains. I was loved and cared for, and I served my person well. She called me her familiar. I would snuggle, purr, and present rodent gifts to show how much I loved her. I helped her relax to hear her inner voice.

When I died, she buried me with ceremony in the back yard. I meowed through the ethers for a full year to let Mommy know how much I missed her, and she heard me. The day a visiting psychic heard me too made Mommy's heart happy.

Portrait of Bandit

A Requiem for Bandit

Shy on funds to pay rent, I gave the second bedroom to a friend of a friend. GeorgiaLyn's house rental had been sold. She gave me first and last months' rent, then moved in with her two cats and a request that I relinquish my art area for her crafts. I explained that she had rented a room with kitchen privileges, not the whole apartment, and that small area was my studio. She seemed stressed, and I understood that the move was hard for her. I hoped she could set up a workspace in her room.

She gave notice at the end of her first month because her parents required a live-in caregiver, and she was the only sibling available. She offered the security deposit and last month's rent if I found a home for her cats. I agreed, and she left her unwanted furnishings with me as well as her pets.

I found a home for the young cat, Neppie; but the older cat was ill. At first, I resented her, eyes hungry for her mistress. Abandoned, sick, a burden, who needed another cat? Her eyes were deep coals that you could sink into and get caught. I told myself, "She's a cat, remember, just an old cat."

Money was lean and she was fat, hungry all the time for expensive food, for some quality loving. She was jealous of my beloved, the cat I chose, the one who chose me.

Hisses, sibling rivalry, adjustments, a truce – then a funny thing happened, I decided to love her. I thought, *What would happen if she got what she needed? Could an old cat learn new tricks?*

Though very old, she healed. Each day alive became a blessing. Bandit blossomed. Her soul was shining; but the body goes its distance. She faded fast when the time came. Yet even at the end, she purred for love.

She pulled herself down the hall, back legs dragging, falling from side to side. I picked her up, fat cat now so frail, skin and bones, ready to go. I laid her on a blanket beside my bed that night. She was gone in the morning.

My chosen cat, Minuit, watched with a curious meow as I buried the abandoned freeloader. Now, beloved Bandit's grave resides beside the rose bush where she lay in the sun to enjoy the garden's beauty.

Angel Bianco

Healer Cat Bianco

Meow meowerer, meow. (translation: *Smell cancer, knead.*)
— Bianco

I joined a coven, the Covenant of the Lunar Cauldron, to expand my knowledge of nature-based religions, in this case, Wicca. Listening to our wise coven leader, I had to accept that twenty-year-old Minuit needed to transition. My cat was holding on to be there for me, and it was time for her to go.

After Minuit died, I decided not to have another pet because of low income. It could happen, but only if a cat just showed up.

Six months later, one of the coven sisters was expecting a baby. She had a cat that wanted a lot of attention, and she needed to find him a good home. I agreed to meet him.

When the couple brought nine-year-old "Bonzo" to my apartment, I suggested he look the place over, and if he wanted to stay, he could. When the expectant couple was ready to leave, Bonzo stayed by my side, having made his choice.

I renamed him because he was a handsome long-haired, white Turkish Angora. Italian *bianco* meant white, and the name was quickly adopted by the cat formerly known as Bonzo. He became a therapy cat, affecting my healing.

Bianco started kneading the groin area when he snuggled in my lap. I had been spotting lightly, so contacted my primary care. CT scans showed nothing, but the spotting continued, as did Bianco's kneading. I detected an unusual odor after a few months and returned to the doctor for a referral.

This time I saw a gynecologist. The scan showed a definite tumor in my uterus, and it was malignant. Medical Detective Bianco stopped his kneading after the hysterectomy.

Thank God

The car was comatose. A truck came barreling down the right lane behind me, another truck on the left.

I prayed, *God take me quickly if it's my time, or start this car!*

I turned the key again, and the car started, dying as soon as I pulled into a turnout around the corner where there was a call box.

When the tow truck arrived, the mechanic observed, "I don't know how you got this car to move. It's dead."

Dragonflies

I was healing heartache, and the balmy breeze caressed my face boating on Loch Lomond. Small dragonflies circled the boat. Inspired, I sang, "Dragonfly, dragonfly, come kiss my hand as you fly by." Then, they congregated on my right hand.

I sang again, "Dragonfly, dragonfly, come kiss my hand as you fly by." From the far-left bank, a large blue dragonfly flew straight toward me. He placed a brief kiss on my right hand and flew off. The group followed him as if he were their guru.

I sensed a lesson as my sadness lifted. Connection can be brief and beautiful, yet when it's over, let go with gratitude, and move on.

Later, a large blue dragonfly teased my cat by charging at him sitting in the bedroom window. The glass protected both as Henri jumped up to catch the shimmering insect. I observed them playing at least three times wondering if that gaming dragonfly was the one that kissed my hand.

Whether he was or not, encounters with dragonflies remind me to be present in the moment. Embrace now.

Things change too fast.

Hot Date

I answered his inquiry from Match.com. He wanted a date in-person. I sent a photo of me when my weight was still 120 pounds, and I felt insecure, even anxious about meeting him. Daring to be brave, I decided to write back, "Yes, where and when."

That Saturday, we met at a local restaurant. When he arrived, I saw that his photo must have been when he was younger and more slender.

I relaxed thinking, "I can eat now without choking."

Crystal Flower

Solitude

Alone
is something I need.
I seek solitude naturally.

Alone
I hear birds express
their need in song.

Alone
I see sunlight glint off water
and sparkle diamonds.

Alone
I feel the breeze
gently stroke leaves.

Alone
I smell the pungent perfume
of flowers seeking sun.

Alone
I can remember.

Melanie on *The Gendron Tarot* Princess of Swords

The Princess of Swords

The "Princess of Swords" card for *The Gendron Tarot* represents courage and the ability to face oneself, to discern one's truth and be real. I desired these characteristics when I placed a modeling photo of me at twenty on the card.

Opportunities presented to develop courage, especially where health was concerned. My body went through a series of challenges – a fall that compacted my back, breast reduction to alleviate back pain, repairing an upper anal fistula, then developing a rectovaginal fistula that required a colostomy. My local surgeon commented that I almost died and referred me to Stanford for the rectovaginal repair.

Beloved daughter, Sandi, took training to be my In-Home Supportive Services (IHSS) caregiver. She was very conscientious, and it made my situation easier having her with me. I relied upon and rallied from her loving care.

I spent four and a half years wearing an ostomy bag to collect intestinal waste. There were numerous proceedures and operations at Stanford Hospital. Then, finally, reconnection and no more bag.

After hospital surgeries, I worked for a local magazine to produce the month's offering, no matter what, to be on top of bills. I often interviewed people, one of whom became a best friend and publisher of some of my books, Elizabeth Porter (Annie), CEO of River Sanctuary Publishing in Felton.

A Pranic Healing practitioner, Annie also became a valued member of my health-care team. She hosted healing groups that included me in their prayers. Their positive support helped me throughout the journey to wellness.

Another friend, Sajohn, chanted songs in Sanskrit that initiated a transcendental state. Bianco sat on my lap to enjoy a taste of Nirvana with me.

Sajohn and I met shortly before he went to India. He returned years later and honored me with the opportunity to design the cover for his book, *Bhagavad-Gita: The Ambrosial 'Sat-Song' of Sri Krishna*.

I've learned that negative emotions like fear and doubt can be mollified with meditation and prayer. At Stanford, after surgeries, I chanted my mantra internally. It helped me cope.

Life is unpredictable. I am grateful for all aspects of my journey. Suffering has blessings if we choose to see them. Admittedly, there are times when it is hard to crawl into the light. Having come close to death, I treasure life every day more than the day before.

Compassion

Cello Phonics

after a cello concert by Diane Frank and Erik Ievins

Stanford Hospital again, surgery successful,
wrapped in Agape by friends
who give me a celebratory concert.

Two cellos harmonize –
rising, falling, soothing chords
with a hint of Tibetan bowls
in the subtext.
Their baritone voices
promise redemption.

Cleansed in the sonic bath,
I feel transformed by
the renewal of music.

It moves through my body
like a psychic chiropractor.
Deep notes of resonance
seed an echo of dreams –
hummingbirds and angels
make joy the dominant emotion.

Patients, nurses, and doctors
fill the room and hall.
Are they receiving this moment's grace?
Do they feel the electric charges
that tingle, enliven, and heal me?

With compassion a blanket,
I feel assured by
the endurance of hope.

The Heart of Dance

Music summons the body to dance.
Multicolored notes emote.
A horn brays like a charging bull.
A cello elicits tears of compassion.
The piano, both static and lyrical,
celebrates the silence between.

Life is an orchestra of sound
perpetuating movement –
light as a bell, heavy as an oboe,
prismatic as a piccolo.

Bach, Beethoven, Brahms,
Tchaikovsky, Rachmaninoff, Grieg,
the Beatles, the Dead, the Doors.

Stroboscopic rhythms enthrall,
pulse blood through veins,
and envelope the senses.

A baby feels its mother's hum
in the rhythm of the rocker.
A child becomes a prima ballerina
waltzing to Blue Danube by Strauss.
Later she responds to rock and roll,
twisting, twirling, timing moves
to the band's beat.

Music becomes dance.
Dance becomes music.
The body's movement
creates a symphony.

Of Byzantium

Number Three Tree

Lightning struck her
antediluvian limbs,
rending her in two,
yet she weathered steadfast.

A sprig before Christ's birth,
she forms an archway
for forest dwellers –

deer, mountain lion, wild turkey,
rabbit, coyote, human –
all gain from her passage
to beauty.

It took a year after I fell
to manage the walk
to Number Three Tree.

Cradled against
her massive trunk,
healing energy
soothed my back
like an
effervescent
water-
fall.

After He Died

Isat in their magical garden, bird pecking at the deck, squirrels darting among trees when I sensed his presence.

My heart melted like the tree moss dangling from oak limbs. I thought, *I love this garden and the life you and your wife created. I wish I could have had more time with you, but I treasure what we did have. You loved my best friend well. I admire the long marriage you shared.*

In the silence I heard, *Did you wish you had an enduring union like ours?*

I replied simply, *Of course.*

Nurturing Forest

Steve and Ruditu

The tuxedo kitten traveled far from his siblings, searching for his lost mother. He wandered onto the driveway where we took notice of him. Query throughout the neighborhood found no one had lost a kitten. He was obviously a stray looking for food, approximately two months of age and apparently healthy. I considered adding another cat, but was unsure I could afford it, so decided to help find him a home.

My friend, Steve, had just lost a tuxedo named Rudi. He adopted the kitten, naming him Ruditu. I met Steve through friend and coven-mate, Mellow. He helped us set up our booths at fairs, and I often hired him to do odd jobs and deliver papers for a local magazine. We laughed a lot.

I trusted Steve to give the kitten a good home knowing he loved cats. He had shown his kindness when he and Mellow cared for me upon release from operations and procedures at Stanford Hospital. Eventually, Steve became my In-Home Support caregiver when my daughter's leukemia made it necessary to seek another.

One rainy evening, after Mellow went home, Steve and I watched a movie. He was younger than me. We had known each other for two years, and I was not looking for a relationship. I am not sure how it happened, but we kissed. Then we kissed again, and again. After he got up to leave, I asked him to stay, and he never left.

Steve and Ruditu joined the household. Turkish Angora, Bianco, the older cat, was very patient when the young one stalked and jumped him regularly. Running down the hall into an open bag provided great pleasure for the black and white cat and his adoring people.

Ruditu was not a cuddly cat. He liked to get outside and hunt, but he did lay by my side and let me stroke his short, silky fur. He' was gone for hours when Steve picked up the hose to water the garden.

We were a family of four for six years until the tuxedo disappeared. Bianco obviously grieved as did we. Ruditu was a wanderer though, and I would wonder where he went.

Perhaps he snuck into a car that drove far away, or he was prey for a wild animal here in the mountains, or perhaps joined a band of traveling gypsies. I like to think he is with someone somewhere who loves him as much as we did.

Ruditu

Henri

He was striking – having an athletic gait and a perfect form with rippling muscles. I called to him, "Who are you? I haven't seen you in my yard before." He stopped, turned, and walked toward me, very sure of himself. I had only the screen slider between us.

I was mesmerized by his gaze, and found myself saying, "Do you want to come in?" Then, I slid the door open.

He entered as if it were his home. Within a month, it was.

Handsome, lithe, ginger,
consummate prancing delight
had me at Meow.

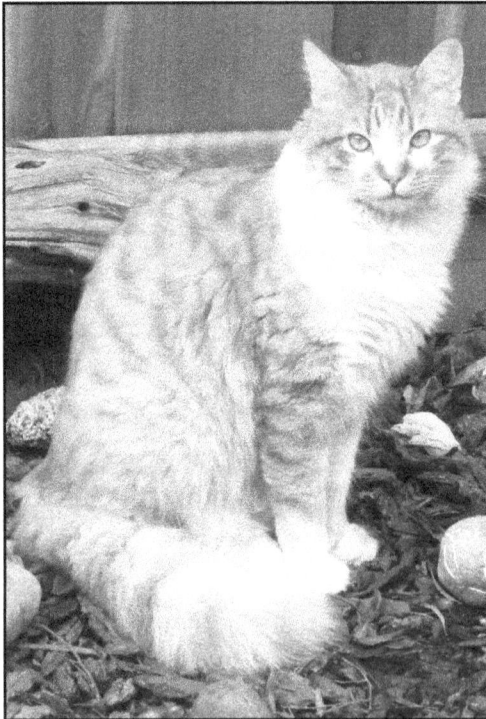

Henri

Henri Finds a Home

I was born a feral stray to a mother who taught me how to hunt vermin and source food in dumpsters. I was free to wander alleys where people who slept on the street gave me treats. One day, I was offered chicken, then picked up and put in a cage.

I clawed, bit, and hissed to break free, but the cage door held. Labeled unadoptable, I was placed in a group of cats destined to live in barns catching vermin. I was rescued to be a mouse catcher for a small goat farm in the mountains where I drank goat milk for the first time.

I roamed the neighborhood freely. Friendly people gave me food and called me handsome. I learned to flick my fluffy tail just so, to make them treat me. Of course, I enjoyed catching mice, but I liked sneaking into the goat keeper's house to snuggle in bed with her daughter. I knew there was a better life waiting for me, even though the goat lady would yell, "You're a barn cat. Get out and do your job."

The day I crossed a yard and was called by a woman standing in the doorway, I stopped and walked up to her with a begging meow. She said I was beautiful, and that she had never seen me before. We both knew she was my person. I visited her every day.

To my great joy, the goat keeper let me stay with her, saying, "Now I'll rescue another cat, one who will be happy to catch vermin. Henri just wants to be a pampered pet."

Being a pet meant learning to follow commands like "no bite," "stay," and "no." I had to come in at night since I now had a home.

I did what was asked because it made my person purr.

Blessing or Gift

No makeup, disheveled hair, lines carved in a once-smooth face, I see a realized woman staring back at me. "We're free now," she says, "to be real. There is no need to impress, just be."

Painting the face electric no longer tempts my vanity. I disposed of all my cosmetics – the lipstick, eyeliners, and various mask-making elements. What need I hide? The wrinkles are evidence of a full life lived. Like the stretch marks from childbirth, they are badges of honor.

O.K. I admit I am not entirely truthful when I say I don't need something to brighten my countenance. I like my hair brushed, teeth clean, and clothing that flatters.

It took me a long time to respect the sacredness of my body, a most wondrous gift, one not to be disowned or denied. It is the vehicle that houses my soul, that spark that makes me divine.

I suspect vanity has a touch of grace within.

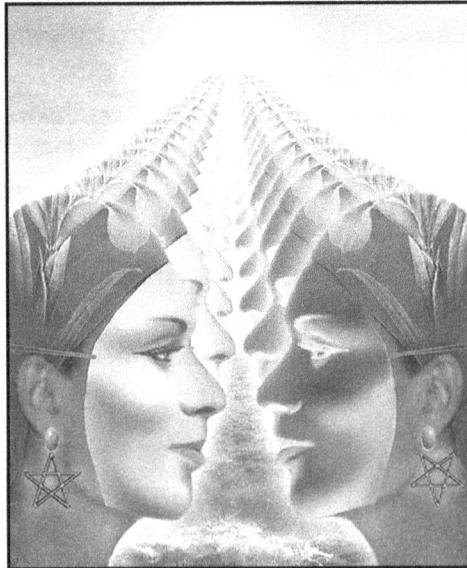

Removing my Mask

Lament of an Elder

My back aches
on the verge of nausea.
Body cells are on fire.
Medications dry me out,
and I'm living on lozenges.
If incontinent today,
I pray it happens at home.

I miss the girl
  who climbed Mount Monadnock –
      breathing the mountain,
  who danced on Martha's Vineyard
      showing fashions in Edgartown,
  who cherished Yoga –
      Bound Lotus and Surya Namaskar,
  who loved to endorphin run,
      do a Flash dance workout,
  and swim like a dolphin.

She's a memory now,
but remembering her
soothes the ache
in an aging body.

Mountain on Fire

Dystopian skies,
blood-red sun,
an alien world has begun.
Fiery landscape surrounds,
orange atmosphere and
black, silhouetted trees
presume apocalypse.
The frightening beauty
whispers prophecy.

Lightning Storm

We are in a heat wave – 106° two days ago, 100° yesterday. It's way too hot today for outdoor activities. Without fans and some cooling, I'm not sure I will survive the lack of air.

We lost power over the last three days. There was a flash thunder and lightning storm that blew out transformers pre-dawn.

I manage asthma with inhalers, but breathing gets labored in extreme heat. I sit here weak, waiting for the lights to go on. Like many seniors, I also take medication to control blood pressure. I am bloated and retaining water. It invites irritability. I feel both crabby and clammy.

Somehow that brings thoughts of the ocean and how lovely it is to soak in cold water. I think I'll just close my eyes and think the sound of waves.

Warning

When I called PG&E at 7:30AM, the robotic voice said that workers were on site, and there would be an update available in four hours. At 4:00PM, I asked my next-door neighbor if he had any news about when we might get our power back. He replied that PG&E expected restoration by 11:45PM – over twenty-four hours without power this time. The explanation, of course, was equipment failure. I fear the world is old and breaking down like me.

Yellow-orange sky, red sun, warnings to evacuate. Lightning struck hundreds of fires throughout California. We are packed and ready to go. A hummingbird is at the feeder, adapting to the new norm of grey smoke.

Evacuation

Living in a town surrounded by forest, fire is a real concern. During the lightning storm, hundreds of fires erupted all over California. Orange sky and blood-red sun intensifies. I realize, "This is serious."

The warning that evacuation was imminent required gathering necessities for an anticipated few days. Cat carrier and cat food, enough clothing for a week, toiletries, medications, books to read, work to do, computer, and then I question, "What do I really want to save?"

I look around the apartment that has served as home and studio for twenty-five years. My heart aches at the thought of losing the original paintings that prove the existence of my art career. I think, *Ultimately, all things must go.*

I decide the treasures that matter most are the beautiful day-dream catchers my deceased daughter created. Embedded with crystals, they send glorious prisms around the room, bringing her spirit to me.

Inspired by a neighbor's call, I pack important papers just in case. Then we get the order for mandatory evacuation.

Steve and I contemplate where to go. He attempts to call his son just as the phone rings telepathically. We're invited to stay in the new guest room, and he, a professional mover, offers to bring a truck to pack up my artwork. I am filled with gratitude that overcomes fear. Happily, we can bring our Norwegian Forest cat who will need to stay inside for the duration.

Exodus

Noah and his partner, Andy, arrive. We've already packed our car with Henri whining in his carrier. We pile paintings into Andy's SUV, and check to make sure we got all the art. She and Noah drive off.

We do a final check. Three favorite paintings get shoved into the back seat with my iMac, Henri, and luggage.

Arriving in San Jose, we settle into our accommodations. We're told paintings have already been unpacked and are in the garage. My gratitude expands.

A distressed Henri meets two adults, three teenagers doing school virtually because of Coronavirus, two cats, two large rabbits, four small bunnies, a bearded lizard, and a coop full of chickens. We are told to make ourselves at home. We are family.

Displaced

Seated in meditation, I listen to the symphony of an oscillating fan. Chickens call out the morning, and a soft moment of calm releases to the angst attempting residence in the pit of my stomach. Will the fire devour our home? Will our garden survive? What about the hummingbirds?

After organizing belongings, Steve asks if I remembered to pack "Ode to Extinction," and I realize all my serigraphs, many original watercolors, and drawings have been left behind. His favorite angel is still on the wall to the right of my bedroom door.

Steve decides to drive home Sunday morning to get needed items only to find all roads into the Santa Cruz mountains are closed. No one is allowed to return. I keep praying for our town, our friends, and our cherished home.

The Waiting Game

I request email updates from CalFire. On the sixth day in San Jose, it looks like it may be another six before we can return home. Roads into the mountains are policed, and citations are possible.

Henri has acclimated enough to hide in closets. He wants to get out even though the resident cats have accepted his presence. One day he tries to climb out via the fireplace. Settling on a ledge, covered in soot, he discovers it is not a valid way out.

He's a wily cat, very intelligent. Andy, who has fostered many cats, said not one of them ever tried to exit by way of the fireplace until Henri. I wish I had a collar for him, though he probably would wiggle out of it.

Everyone is kind, understanding that we are stressed. My attachment to our cat is possibly laughable as I walk through the house on occasion calling to my hidden feline, fearing that he got out.

I pray, I meditate, I work. Andy gets a donated desk for me to set up my computer. A book arrives for me to design, and I feel myself relaxing into our new, hopefully temporary norm.

The latest news tells us the perimeter of Felton is secure, and our town should fare well. UCSC and Scotts Valley residents can return home. Most homes in the valley are without power, and two water pipes melted in the fire, leaving homes above Brookdale without water.

After ten days, I finally fall apart. Steve needs a break, and plans to drive to Davenport for a day on the beach.

I break into tears, not wanting to be without him. Then I realize I am a survivor and wish him a healing beach day. He leaves only to return an hour later to say, "The roads remain closed, even to Davenport."

Back Home

The evacuation orders lift. The smoke initiates asthma. We have power. Henri reacquaints himself with favorite lounging spots.

Our garden survived somewhat. Two nights of rain helped slow the fire. Fire folk reside in Henry Cowell Park while fighting the CZU Lightning fire.

Noah brings back my art. We hang paintings. I set up my computer, and life returns to a shaky normal with a 106° heat. Global warming is painfully evident.

Fire season started early while we sheltered at home due to Coronavirus. The CZU Lightning Complex Incident Fact Sheet listed 86,509 acres burned, 925 residences, 171 commercial, and 388 minor structures destroyed. We have deep gratitude for the firefighting heroes who saved our town.

It's 3:30PM. The sky is a dark, deep orange. I tell Henri that the sky changed color to honor his orange tabby coat. He just licks his paw.

The Elements

Stormy Holiday

Barking thunder, a lightning flash, and my adrenalin was pumping while gathering rosemary for the holiday meal. I called out, "Henri, come home," as I ran to the house. When I opened the door, hail battered the garden.

For the next few stormy hours, I called for him often, fearing his frightful demise.

The downpour softened to light rain, and my wanderer returned, completely dry.

While I cried, he had sheltered nearby.

That cat is smarter than I am.

Birds Watching

Deep Grey Agape

A shadow of despair has
permeated the neighborhood.
Houses keep losing power.
Even the mice are hiding.

In the news –
earthquakes topple buildings,
and the voices in the rubble
fall silent.

Making pain a mantra,
I pray that humankind
takes the leap to love
one another.

Nepthys

Gaia's Tears

I saw Gaia's tears erupt:
    fire,
    flood,
    quake.

The world shook:
    falling rocks,
    avalanche,
    crumbling ice,

the globe warming
to destruction.

Who will save us
when we fall?

Will Jesus take
our hand?

A Domestic Feline Manifesto

We House Cats, in order to obtain a more perfect existence, establish just care, have domestic tranquility, provide for our common good, promote our general welfare, and secure the blessings of freedom for ourselves and our kittens, do ordain and establish this manifesto for all domestic felines.

Article 1: Cats do not apologize for being adorable. It is our inalienable right as feline freeloaders to finagle a place in a human's heart. We are each meant to be irresistible. This is a domestic cat's calling.

Article 2: Each kitten must learn to play with squeaky toys. Humans like the irritating noise these playthings make. Why else would they give them to us? It is of paramount importance to entertain humans to acquire food, shelter, and adoration.

Article 3: Once a home is secured, a cat must remain charming. Rolling over and presenting one's belly to rub is mandatory, especially after running away from our human when we are not ready to come home.

Article 4: No matter how much our human gets attached, we are free to make up our own minds. We can eat catnip, flick our tails, rub our human's legs, and snuggle when we want.

Article 5: It is our right to play with our prey and then bring it home as a gift to our human.

Article 6: Indoor-only cats must be free to scratch furniture, meow loudly, and do what is necessary to get their human's attention to acquire what is desired.

Article 7: We must remember – bad cats get kicked out; good cats get treats.

Signed: Collage, Minuit, Bianco, Ruditu, Henri

The Vast Quiet

In the hour of long shadows, owls wait for the moon.
Dawn's hush invites night dwellers to awaken,
hungry and ready to hunt.

Fear eats the heart like vultures devour carrion.
Faith alone protects one who wanders
the dark forest alone.

There is an abyss between mountains,
where a yodel could not find its home
no matter how hard it tried to reach an ear.

A buzz of flies circle in the still
hot air that parches the throat,
leaving dust behind.

Promises are oaths to betray,
yet silence reigns in a fearful heart.
There will be no love today.

Vague pictures present as memories
not quite forgotten – ghosts
that persist through time.

Turning from the vast landscape,
I see a hawk in search of sustenance,
its eye on the ground.

Who goes there in the desert heat
beneath a canopy of stone?
Who walks the valley like a lizard?

What Now?

I dream of darkness and fear dying. My aunt has a heart episode, landing overnight in the hospital. A week of uncertainty tests my confidence.

I want to write a perfect poem or a story worth telling. I desire my best, but words elude a mind with thoughts chasing around like overactive ferrets.

My inner parent lifts me from depression, offers positive discourse. She calms me with meditation and affirmative prayer. She says simply, "Have faith."

Grateful for my resilient self, I decide to write a micro-memoir.

My ninety-six-year-old aunt Lorraine
died this week, leaving me
as the last living generation.

Mermaid

Ruminating with Henri

Henri stares at me. His steady eyes call forth my truth. They ask, "What now? What do you want?"

I reply, "I want – quiet, peace, kindness – to give and receive. This world struggles with judgement and hatred for anyone not agreeing or associated with one's group. I see too much division in government – us against them. War, hate crimes, and mass shootings crowd the news."

Pensive Henri seems to wonder, *Is there any hope?*

I pontificate further, "There's always hope. It helps to maintain faith in good overcoming evil. I believe the need to know our divine nature is embedded in human DNA. We desire to know how, why, and who we truly are."

Henri curls up in my lap, and the drone of my voice puts him to sleep. He enjoys my petting, and as he purrs, I continue my internal discourse. "We experience suffering: heartache, mental stress, physical challenges, world angst, and more in this life. It's how we respond that develops our souls – light or dark, innocent or cognoscente – we become what we choose."

I look at my sleeping feline and am in awe of his beauty. No earthly scientist or artist could design such a perfect creature.

I say to Henri, "You prove the existence of God."

Henri

If Only I Could Replay that Day

It was the first dry day after a three-day power outage storm. Our car died the week before, and we decided to begin our search for another. We borrowed a friend's truck and drove to town.

Having owned Toyotas and Hondas, we visited the Toyota dealership first. A charming smile preceded a young man with hungry eyes, "May I help you?"

Conversation ensued, and we listed our wants, including monthly payments of no more than $300. The young man's eyes turn hopeful. Three hours looking at available used cars begins with the first being a Toyota Camry. The seats comfortably support my injured back, "I really like this."

The young man's smile widens. He brings us to the manager to discuss terms. I emphasize the low monthly payments, and the manager says, "I am sure we can help you. I'll be back as soon as I crunch some numbers." It's beyond our means. We're ready to leave when the manager insists, "We have cars within your budget. Don't leave yet."

The young man gathers a Chevy for us to try. I sit in the passenger seat and my back goes out. "This won't do." My partner squirms. Three cars later, we are shown a sleek black Toyota Corolla. The passenger seat is comfortable.

The manager reassures us the Corolla fits our budget at $300 a month with a down payment of $4,000. We are ushered into the finance office, and an exhausting hour later, we have purchased a car for $350 a month and $4,000 down.

I explain I will come back the next day with cash for the down payment as it is at home. The young man offers to drive the Corolla to our house to save us an extra trip to town. He emphasizes, "We'll collect the down payment and conclude the sale." His assistant follows to be his ride back.

I am eighty, and by now, worn out. "O.K."

The next day, I receive notice my rent has increased by $300 a month. I study the sales paperwork to find the monthly car payment went from $300 to $350 because of an unwanted maintenance contract being added. I follow procedure and request that it be removed from the contract. I am reassured a check will be sent to my bank within six to eight weeks. A year passes without remuneration and at least three certified mail requests. My cousin who used to sell cars had warned me not to go to a dealership. Warning – heavy duty salesmen can wear down a senior.

Oh well, I really liked our car named Raven, but If I could redo that sale day, I would not have purchased her. She was a little low for my old legs to climb into. Knees and hips were crying, and I wished I had a different vehicle, maybe a RAV4 like my friend, Annie.

On a Friday afternoon, on his way back from the beach, Steve pulled onto Hwy 1 misjudging the distance of an oncoming car. He was hit, the car totaled. At Dominican ER they found bruised ribs, one fractured. Raven, the Black Sand Pearl Toyota Corolla that we had only eighteen months, was dead.

Thank God, Steve was alive. His lesson was patience. He drove cautiously after the accident, making sure the road's clear before entering.

I learned a few things from this experience. First, have good insurance. Mine paid off the loan, and Toyota paid what was due me. Research before shopping, know what you want and can afford, take time, look around, and be brave enough to say "No." If you're tired, go home, and be careful with your wishes.

Annie decided to upgrade her vehicle, so I bought Silverstreak, her Toyota RAV4.

In My Room

I watch my cat
watch hummingbirds
through the bedroom window.

Beside the birdfeeder,
the hanging geranium has
fewer purple flowers,
her tendrils brittle in fall.

In summer, my pungent rose
lasted only a few days.
Petals turned pink to blush,
then brown. In decay,
some scent remained.

At night, blanketed in darkness,
I remember the smell of roses
and the brief shimmer of
wings in the waning sun.

Air

Revelation

The world is drowning in fire,
drought, flood, war,
pandemic, loss, fear.

There is a movement
of revelation
in the atmosphere.

Will the Horsemen
take us on a ride
to Armageddon?

On the other side
lives the unknown –
to be discovered.

Noah's Ark

Why Can't We

Why can't we
conduct ourselves
as citizens of a country
where compassion
supersedes greed?

Why can't we
unite the divide
and mend
the torn tapestry
of the politically correct?

Why can't we
compromise as friends,
and seek the best solution
for problems
when they arise?

Why can't we
choose to serve
rather than consume,
care for one another
as we care for ourselves –

Why can't we?

On Awakening Gratitude

The grey dawn slowly brightened
with strands of sun
breaking through blinds
streaming across the bed,
onto the still-cold floor.

Life felt distant,
having hibernated through
a long, dark winter,
deep in the snow of slumber
longing to laugh.

And black was soothing,
a loving blanket that
wrapped warm the soul,
getting past months of bed rest
and wanting to run.

The light demands action,
days dreaming blossoms
and a harvest of love –
the health of body,
mind, spirit and soul.

Of course there is suffering.
Experience is a journey for
the witness to embrace,
yet what we are grateful for
far outweighs the challenge.

The Endurance of Hope

Lifelong friends, having shared nearly a hundred years together, relaxed around the firepit sipping wine. The late afternoon sun streamed through trees laden with dangling moss in the magical garden. They watched hummingbirds flutter the bird feeder sipping nectar. A mother rabbit and bunny peeked out from behind the agave, listening intently when Dee inquired, "How do you feel, Mellie, on this, your hundredth birthday?"

"Happy to be alive! I had hoped to make it to one hundred, and I endured. Remember how in my seventies, I had the desire to live a century plus? Well, here I am. Light enters my room every morning, calling my spirit to actively embrace the day."

"I love your latest book on the *New York Times* best sellers list, *Art Is Life; Life Is Art*. Knowing you all these years, I am confident this book is memoir-based."

Melanie thought before replying, "Like anyone's life, mine has been filled with bumps, bruises, and outrageous joy. I drew from this to develop the character of Aurora. She struggles in a patriarchal society to create her art and thrive. Like me, she was born at the end of World War II. Military hoopla filled the atmosphere. Aurora's father, like my Papa, had served in the United States Navy and the French Foreign Legion.

"Rita was Papa's oldest daughter, and she was my mother. I used that part of my life experience to create the tension Aurora felt with men. Like me, she kept searching for her never-to-be-met father. I was told he most likely died in the war, everything about him was a mystery until DNA testing as an adult revealed he was a European Jew. And yes, of course that is autobiographical."

Dee's memory was slipping, "I know you told me the story before, but tell me again how you discovered that, and how it affected you."

Melanie reminisced, "Papa died in my seventh year. At the wake, my oldest sister held me tightly saying I could now come live with her. I asked Mama why she said that and was told my sister was really my mother. Mama and Papa adopted their first grandchild because Rita was not able to care for me.

"She was movie star beautiful, just like your mother, Dee. Men adored her Bohemian nature which complicated her life. I'm an artist, married numerous times, part of the Love Generation, a bit of a Bohemian myself. It's obvious my mother's blood is in my veins."

Dee sipped her wine, "Looking back at your life's hard-earned lessons, what words of wisdom come to mind?"

Melanie smiled, "The last twenty years have really been the best. My career continues to flourish, and I enjoy cherished sister friendships, especially ours. Steve has been a loving partner for thirty-five years now. We both love animals, having rescued many cats.

"Remember Minuit? She was my little familiar. Bianco, the sweet healer, followed with tuxedo Ruditu joining the family. Henri was the best feral, training more like a dog. My Bedlington, Beatle, was a cherished companion. I could go on, but you are aware of my love for creatures.

"Perhaps I would not have divorced three times if I had treated husbands as pets. I loved my pets unconditionally, accepting and forgiving their trespasses. As I think about it, some of my most satisfying relationships have been with animals."

The wind carried a chill as evening descended. With her ninth English Setter, Aslan, settled at her feet, Dee gathered a shawl around her shoulders, "Happy Birthday, Mellie. Let's hope you make it to one hundred one."

Melanie as Fairie Godmother

Acknowledgements

Thank You to those who helped birth this book:

Deep gratitude for Diane Frank, author, poet, mentor, and friend. Her poetry, memoir, and flash fiction workshops encouraged invention, amplifying creative expression. Diane's and the group's feedback vastly improved my writing skills. The majority of poems and stories in this book were either written or begun in Diane Frank's workshops.

Thank you, Erik Ievins, for expert editing.

I also thank the friends and family who listened and offered their honest critiques of my writing in progress. You helped me refine this book – Annie, Dee, Paola, Paula, and Steve.

This book could not be what it is without beloved pets – Collage, Bird, Mousekin, Beatle, Minuit, Bianco, Ruditu, and Henri.

These stories and poems appeared in the following:

"A Later Dive at Point Lobos," "Beginning Life Mastery 101," "Christ Light," "Jai Guru Dev, Maharishi," "Sweat Lodge," *This Fool's Journey through Tarot's 22 Major Arcana*, Blue Light Press, 2014

"On Awakening Gratitude," anthology, *River of Earth and Sky: Poems for the Twenty-First Century*, Blue Light Press, 2015; *Dreaming the Light*, River Sanctuary Publishing, 2018

"Healer Cat Bianco," as "Bianco, Cat Extraordinaire," *Making the Connection to Self, Love, Life*, River Sanctuary Publishing, 2016

Melanie on *The Gendron Tarot* IX The Hermit

About the Author

Living artfully, with integrity, guides my life.
I seek to express Truth in personal vision,
to communicate honestly with consideration,
committed to excellence in all endeavors.
I choose to be real.

– Melanie Gendron

Melanie Gendron attended The School of the Museum of Fine Arts, Boston in affiliation with Tufts University, majoring in sculpture and painting. Studies in photography, print making, fashion design and computer arts further rounded out her curriculum.

She developed a unique style rich in symbolism inspired by many cultures. Proficient in a variety of media, Melanie enjoys a renaissance attitude. Serving as animator, art director, author, book designer, fashion designer, graphic artist, illustrator, intuitive counselor, poet, painter, portraitist, teacher, and writer, she is a seasoned multimedia professional artist.

Among her publications are *A Goddess Journal, Making The Connection to Self, Love, Life, The Gendron Tarot Deck and Book, This Fool's Journey Through Tarot's Major Arcana, Dreaming The Light, Metatron, Angel of The Presence,* and *A Goddess Coloring Book.*

Melanie currently manages Gendron Studios in the Santa Cruz Mountains of California, creating her art, and offering commercial art services, specializing in book design.

melaniegendron999@gmail.com

Publications

The Gendron Tarot, book and deck, U.S. Games Systems, 1997

This Fool's Journey Through Tarot's Major Arcana, Blue Light Press, 2014

From River Sanctuary Publishing:

A Goddess Journal, 2015; *Making the Connection to Self, Love, Life*, 2016;

The Elemental Goddess, 2017; *Dreaming the Light*, 2018;

Metatron, Angel of The Presence, 2019;

A Goddess Coloring Book – Art Honoring the Divine Feminine, 2023

Gaia, The Universe

Save a life; adopt a pet.

www.ingramcontent.com/pod-product-compliance
Lightning Source LLC
Chambersburg PA
CBHW022157080426
42734CB00006B/468